DAYS
OF
PRAISE

GRACE JUBILEE

WESTBOW
PRESS®
A DIVISION OF THOMAS NELSON
& ZONDERVAN

WestBow Press books may be ordered through booksellers or by contacting:

WestBow Press
A Division of Thomas Nelson & Zondervan
1663 Liberty Drive
Bloomington, IN 47403
www.westbowpress.com
844-714-3454

Jubilee, Grace.
Days of praise / Grace Jubilee.—First edition.
iv, 85 p. ; 24 cm.
Summary: "Fasting and praising Jehovah are powerful habits in a Christian's life. *Days of Praise* is a program to unite Christians in fasting and worship of our Lord."
1. Christian life. 2. Prayer—Christianity. 3. Fasting—Religious aspects—Christianity. 4. Devotional literature. 5. Devotional calendars. 6. Religion—Christian life—Devotional. I. Grace Jubilee. II. Days of Praise.
242.2

Cover Design by Grace Jubilee

ISBN: 978-1-6642-2557-2 (sc)
ISBN: 978-1-6642-2556-5 (e)

Print information available on the last page.

WestBow Press rev. date: 04/21/2021

CONTENTS

INTRODUCTION

It seems that our country is polluted with sin, distress, and strife. We have become so comfortable with the freedoms that our elders won that we expect safety and righteousness to tend to themselves.

This isn't the first time that the world has been rampant with strife. Evil never gives up, never tires, pushes ever forward. We must do the same. God is still able and willing to change everything.

Christians shrug saying, "What can ya do?" then walk on; turning away from their duties and responsibilities.

I don't remember God saying,

> 'Get saved, then lounge around until you die.'

Is that your moto?

Christians are not helpless.

We have power in the name of Jesus by the blood of Jesus.

When we consider changing our society the idea is overwhelming. Thankfully we do not have to fight every sinful person, corrupt business, or bad law.

We are Christians. We are powerful warriors who fight against evil spirits.

Are you tired of evil taking our children, our culture, our nation?

> Want to do something about it?

A PLAN OF ACTION

We have the power to defeat evil. We are sleeping giants. Each of us.

Just how long is our nap?

More than any other action, the Bible tells us to praise God.

Let us lift high our praises to Yahweh who gives us power and victory over evil.

We know that God loves the praises of his people and some evil can only be defeated with prayer and fasting.

So, let's do it. Let's fast one day per month and on that day, we will offer praise to God.

I see the look of horror and panic on your face.

FAST?! ONE DAY? **EVERY** MONTH??!

You claim to be willing to die for Christ but you can't give up a couple of meals?

Consider your ways.
Consider your devotion.
Consider your eternity.

Days of the Month

For this part of the program each day of the month is given a concept over which we will fast and give praise.

Consider everything that your subject touches or all of the ways that your subject can be viewed. No topic is one dimensional. All topics will overlap.

During the month pray and declare victory over your subject.

On your praise day, fast and only praise God for your subject.

When you pray and praise, don't say the negative. Only declare the victory. Too often we pray against rather than for. Praise God for a resolved, holy situation.

Focus on what God can do. Praise him for what he will do.

For each subject I have brainstormed some ideas and relationships to the subject. They are not intended to be the only or the all of that subject. Use these points to get you thinking beyond the surface or one-dimensional. Challenge yourself to think of the depths and layers of which your subject connects to other principles and concepts.

Seek Yahweh to give you a deeper understanding of your topic.

I've given some examples of praise prayers to get you started. Ask God to give you a direction of spiritual prayer and praise. Declare victory in prayers of praise.

States of Praise

A second part of the plan is that each state is given a week of the year. During that week the residents of that state will declare righteousness and victory for their state. Plan programs and activities that lift up your state in praise to Jehovah.

Events

There are suggestions for events, programs, or ways of using praise. Ask God to show you ways of affecting your city or state for righteousness and holiness.

Scriptures and Knowledge

I don't know all wisdom or answers therefore I can't give them to you. We each must know the Bible for ourselves; for our own souls. Don't depend on someone else's understanding or belief about God.

Learn about Jesus for yourself. Increase your wisdom, knowledge, and understanding. Study the Bible every day.

Today I am praising Jehovah for you. I thank Yahweh for every Christian, for every Bible, for every opportunity to give praise to God.

A FEW WORDS

About Fasting

It seems when people talk about fasting that the most difficult concept to overcome is the time of midnight.

When I have fasted from midnight to midnight, I was so absorbed in the time that I lost focus for the reason about which I was fasting. I had to stay up late, eat in the middle of the night, then was tired tomorrow, and so on. This neither encouraged me to fast, nor did I get much out of it. I easily found all manner of reasons to not fast.

Somehow, I don't think God's power is limited by the rotation of an arrow on the face of a device; that was designed by a human scientist; that allows multiple humans to arrive at a location at the same moment.

God reminded me that the spirit of the fast is more important than the time of day. I humbly suggest that just as Jesus is Lord of the Sabbath, he is also Lord of the fast.

Perhaps, if you fast from and to a time that is less confining you might be more successful. For example, if you fast from sunrise to sunrise, or from supper today until supper tomorrow, you might find that you spend very little time worrying about food and more time focusing on God.

Throughout the day, as my body complains, I remind myself that I will be able to eat at 6 o'clock and that isn't so far away. I then re-dedicate my attention and my praise on God and my fasting subject. I use temptation as a bell that signals me to declare victory and to focus my praise. Now, fasting is a time of victory!

> Ain't no clock gonna keep me from the power of fasting.

Fasting strengthens our resolve and spirit. When we fast, we separate body from soul. It teaches us how to refuse temptation giving us power to choose God over human; righteousness over sin.

Choosing to fast shows a willingness to go against established routines. It trains us to deny impulses and physical desires; altering behavior for spiritual goals. Fasting hones and sharpens our spiritual focus so that we are more prepared when fighting for righteousness.

About Praising

Fasting and praise days are for praise and worship only. No ordering, asking, or begging.

Newsflash God knows that a situation is unrighteous. He doesn't need us to explain it.

More News He knows that we are upset, confused, and afraid.

Guess What Else? God doesn't need us to tell him who is doing what.

And He does not require our great wisdom to explain to him how to resolve a situation.

Don't tell God what to do.

Praise him for his wisdom and power over the situation, then praise him for a resolved situation that is full of righteousness.

What he expects from us is worship. If we don't the rocks will.

Ain't no rock gonna do my duty.

Ain't no rock gonna get my God-given power.

When we praise him, we gain power over temptation; power over fear; power over evil.

On your praise day only worship God. Worship. Sing songs. Declare victory. Only praise. Fasting days are praise days.

Can't think of any praises? Fortunately, the Bible is full of them. Write down praises as you come across them in the Bible. Make note cards listing praises from the Bible. Carry around a few, post them around your car, the office, on your calendar, even in your wallet – there's nothing like praising God to curb impulse buying!

Your Fasting and Praise Day

Search the Bible for scriptures that pertain to your topic. Study God's commandments about your topic.

Praise God for holiness within your subject. Praise Jehovah for the defeat of evil in your subject.

Brainstorm ideas and concepts that interact with your subject. Be creative; be far reaching.

Every topic is multi-dimensional and multi-tiered. No subject is an island. Every concept touches everyone around the earth every day.

Practice writing praise-only prayers. Turn negative prayers into positive ones. Don't tell God what is wrong, praise him for what is right. When you believe that there is nothing positive to say, then thank God for his power and wisdom.

Post praise prayers around your house, in the car, or at work to keep you praising throughout the day. Fall asleep praising God, you'll rest better.

Praise Groups

Do you ever notice that when you commit acts of righteousness you suddenly have problems coming at you from many places? Evil never works alone. Why are you fighting alone?

You need praise buddies. No, this is not your Sunday School group or your social set. Don't meet up with people with whom you already have established patterns or history. Try mixing with nearby congregations and persons outside your daily life. Adding the same ingredients to a dish in a different order will not alter the result nor will swapping the same chairs around the same table.

This group will support you by praising God about you. They tell God all of the reasons that you are a blessing.

For example:
Thank you, Jehovah, that she is strong enough to resist temptation and to treat others with patience and compassion.
You have made him a marvelous Christian full of wisdom and generosity.
They are going through this problem with an abiding joy from you that reveals your mercy, faithfulness, and incredible peace through them.

HALLOWED GROUND

We have neglected a vital practice in our daily walk. Hallowing.

When was the last time that you marked the blood of Jesus... anywhere? How long since you anointed anything with oil?

Hallow wherever you are reading this right now.

This country, this nation, this people belong to Yahweh and we declare them as holy ground marked with the blood of the Messiah in the name and power of Christ Jesus our Lord and savior.

Hallow Your Home

Can't figure out why evil has so much power in your family? Mark the blood of Jesus over your house. Anoint your home.

Do it now.

Every day declare holiness over your home and family.

Hallow Your Church

Our churches face constant attacks from the enemy. The blessings on our churches and staff must be renewed daily. *This is holy ground.*

Hallow Your Job

As you go to work mark the blood of Jesus over your workstation and all that you do. Declare your company for holiness; for righteousness; for Yahweh. Praise over your job, over all that your job and company touches, over the owners, the board of directors, over every branch, every product, every customer.

As you enter or leave place the blood of Jesus over the doorways.

God sees it, so does the enemy.

Hallow Daily

Hallow everywhere you go.

At a restaurant while others are saying grace you are hallowing the business; praying over the owners and the staff.

Everyone who comes in contact with this place I mark with the blood of Jesus.
Lord have mercy on them today. Touch their souls with your purity.
Let them feel your love and desire your grace.

Hallow three places every day. Visit a neighbor and quietly hallow their house. Walk your neighborhood hallowing with every step. As you drive through town hallow. In every thing, every where hallow.

Hallow Your State

Mark the blood of Jesus over your city and state. Declare your state to be holy ground.

My city serves Jehovah. The Messiah is praised in this land.
Evil has no power in our nation, in our country.

This is hallowed ground!

STATES OF PRAISE

For this part of our plan praise and pray over your state during a specific week of the year. This will be a week to declare your state for Jehovah.

Give praise for your state. Declare holiness in your government and your people. Pray over town halls, inside courtrooms, over the streets of your town.

Travel to the state capital. Ask public officials to allow a group from your church to pray with them. Pray over their office, praise over their influence, their power, and their actions. Hallow and declare holiness over their authority and power. Mark the doorpost of their offices, the foundation of their power, with the blood of Jesus.

Pin up a map of your state, county, or town. Each day mark the section over which you pray, so that at the end of the week you have named every street, neighborhood, or town.
Lift up praises over the people in your city or state each day.

Have a walk-about. With a group of Christians, walk every street and road in a town or county. Praise over your state. Make sure, that if you might obstruct traffic, to speak to the appropriate authorities for permits. Of course, do not trespass on any private property, public streets only.

Give thanks and praise for resources, features, industries, and the people in your state. Give praise for your state's future.

Again, we are not asking, directing, or telling Yahweh what to do. We are worshiping him in the name of our state. We praise Jehovah in the name of those who don't believe or don't know him.

> *We declare this place as hallowed ground. This state belongs to God.*
> *We serve Yahweh.*
> *The people of this state choose Jehovah.*
> *This is hallowed ground.*
> *The Messiah reigns in my state.*

Go to Washington. Travel with a group from your church, county, or state.

Hallow the White House.

Call your Senators and Representatives to arrange for meetings and tours of Congress. Pray over the staff, Senators, Representatives, over their authority and duties, hallow their ground. Praise Jehovah in Congress.

The Supreme Court has tours and a gallery. Attend a court case and praise God every moment that you are there. Hallow the ground of the Supreme Court of the United States of America. *The laws of Yahweh reign and govern this country.*

Pray over the power that rules this nation. Give praise over the people who make decisions that affect our country. Declare holiness for our people; mark the doorposts of our nation with the blood of Jesus.

Let our prayers for our nation be continuously lifted up to heaven.

In my state
Of my nation
With my people
Jesus is our Messiah!
Hallelujah!

EVENTS AND PROGRAMS

There are many wonderful programs already in use throughout the country. Here are a few event ideas, some new and some that are modified specifically to praise.

Be sure to acquire any permits or permissions any time you are going to be on private or public property or might interfere with the flow of traffic.

Try to put together a committee from as many churches as possible in your city, county, or state. Whenever possible coordinate programs and events with all churches in your area. Always seek multi-denominational opportunities. You might be a source of support or example that a person's church isn't providing. We unite in Christ.

Praise Days
Host a day of praise in your area. Encourage all churches in your county to have a picnic, breakfast, or open house where anyone can come and receive prayer. You can invite all or have specific themes, such as public officials, those convicted of a crime, medical staff, or news and media to come to be prayed over.

Praise Cloths
Praise over, then give out praise cloths, ribbons, braided wrist bands, and so on in your area. The cloth doesn't have power. It's merely a reminder of God's miracles, your love and prayers; an encouragement and comfort.

Praise In
Have an all night or weekend Praise In. Give praise and worship to God all night at your church, a local park, or pitch in with other churches in your area to rent an arena and invite the whole county or state. Sing songs, worship, read praises aloud from the Bible. Praises only.

Praise Day Group Meetings
Invite anyone in your area to a Bible study for your subject. Find scriptures that relate to your subject. Discuss ways that our society is victorious in this area. Discuss common beliefs and ideas about Christ in relation to the subject. Consider ways that you can affect your community in relation to your subject.

Praise Caroling
Why is caroling limited to Christmas? Sing his praises around your community. Sing praises at the mall, walking through neighborhoods, at parks, in nursing homes, on the steps of a

court or capital, in the library, at festivals and city events, or at tourist attractions. Be creative. Let his praises sound!

Praise Points
Have a praise service at city overlooks, the road into and out of town, teen hangouts, center of town, and so on. Make key points of your community places of praise.

Jericho Walk
Walk around your community or main streets shouting praises to the Lord.

Praise Booth
Set up a booth at local festivals, in malls, hospitals, at sporting events, at parades, or in community centers, where anyone can walk up and receive prayer and praise over them.

Praise Visits
Visit nursing homes or prisons to praise over the people who are there. They need praises spoken over them.

Hallow Hopping
Choose a type of place, such as court houses, barber shops, parks, churches, or downtown, then go from place to place all around the city praising God and hallowing those places.

Christian Karaoke
At your town's next festival host a karaoke contest of Christian songs.

Praise Plays in the Park
Host Christian plays or concerts in your local park.

Praise Walks
Gather to walk while praising Yahweh all day or night. Pledge to walk-in-praise certain hours of the event.

Praise in Public
Challenge all Christians in your area to give praise to our savior in a public place.

Praise-a-Thon
This can be a coordinated effort between cities, states, or regions. Set up a stage in a park or arena and have groups of people sing praises to God continually for a period of time. Every hour of the day and night songs and praises will be sung to Jehovah. When your time is up, handoff to the next town or county who will keep the praises rolling. *This country praises Yahweh.*

Hours of Praise
Host a praise week or month for your county or state. Individuals, families, or churches sign up to praise God during specific hours. *We are Christians. We worship Yahweh.*

Praise Reports
Take out ads in newspapers and magazines, on the radio, or television. The spots should feature folks praising God about his great works, his miracles, his mercy.

Praise Trip
Drive, take a train, plane, or boat and praise God over all that you see. Declare this to be hallowed ground. Declare Jesus as the Messiah over this nation.

Praise Parade
Host a parade or build a float to parade through town singing and shouting praises to the Messiah.

Praise Relay
Runners and walkers carry a cross while running across the city or state handing-off the cross of Jesus from runner to runner.

Neighborhood or Block Praise Party
Host a praise party in your area. This is a time for sharing what God does for us and how wonderful it is to live in Christ.

Border Walk
Walk, drive, sail, or fly the borders of your state or city praising Jesus the whole way.

Praise Line
Stretch hand to hand, person to person, across your county or state praising Jehovah. Challenge neighboring states to meet you at the border. Let's go for a record of the longest praise line ever.

Praise Records
Challenge a neighboring city or state to a contest to see who can have the most people in one place praising Yahweh at one time. *Let the praises of his people be heard in the heavens.*

Notes

_____

_____

_____

_____

_____

_____

_____

_____

_____

_____

_____

_____

_____

_____

_____

_____

_____

_____

_____

Notes

_____

_____

_____

_____

_____

_____

_____

_____

_____

_____

_____

_____

_____

_____

_____

_____

_____

_____

DAYS OF THE MONTH

I AM THE LORD YOUR GOD
Day 1

Our first commandment is to recognize that Yahweh is our God, yet he gives us the choice to serve or ignore him. He will save us, only, if we ask him to.

God's ways are of heaven while we see only the earth. We live in physical form feeling the pull of gravity to the earth each moment.

We search the Bible and history for examples of his methods and precepts. It seems we're all searching for something. People from around the world ask why we are here. We are created like him but struggle to connect and identify with him.

Adam and Eve walked in the garden with Yahweh, now we walk with Jesus. He completes our human soul.

Why did God call himself I AM? Holiness is, righteousness is, purity is. What was holy a thousand years ago will still be holy in another thousand. Purity is unchanged, righteousness cannot be altered. I AM is the same.

Praise Prayers

Holy is the Lamb of God. You are holiness, righteousness, and purity.

You are God of all the earth. Thank you that this nation, our country, chooses you as our God. As for me and my nation we serve the Lord. As for me and my country, we praise Jehovah.

Thank you, Jesus, for leaving heaven to rescue us from hell.

We thank you for your faithfulness and kindness for us. Thank you for the mercy and forgiveness that you give to all who ask.

You reveal yourself to us and to all people everywhere. Our people turn away from other religions. All peoples recognize false gods for what they are.

Your presence is in every aspect of our society. We give you praise continually. You reveal yourself to us every day. We worship a God who loves us. You are our guide, our savior, our redeemer. We praise you.

Those who worship you have joy and peace. We dedicate our souls to you. We give you all praise and worship.

You answer all who call on you. You are our God. Yahweh is holy; our creator; all powerful.

Notes

_____

_____

_____

_____

_____

_____

_____

_____

_____

_____

_____

_____

_____

_____

_____

_____

_____

_____

_____

_____

_____

Notes

GRAVEN IMAGE
Day 2

Jehovah's power is infinite and that scares us. God is the ultimate unknown. We can't see him or touch him. Though we may call out to him, we only hear him when he allows. We only know of him what he chooses.

It's unsettling to realize that this being has complete control and power over us; over all the earth.

If we were to have an image of God, then we would believe that he is a known quantity. We then imagine that we can learn his powers, mitigate risks, and eventually overpower him. Statuettes, pictures, and the like offer an illusion of a being that is limited and controllable.

Further, carved and drawn images can be altered and manipulated to suit the artist's preference. Images can be interpreted and translated into a new meaning and intent. Soon the current image bears little resemblance to the original.

I AM is unchanging.

Wisdom starts with recognizing God's power. The beginning of peace is accepting that Yahweh truly loves us.

Praise Prayers
. . . .

Thank you, Yahweh, for revealing yourself to us. Thank you for your constant presence that reassures us of your love and compassion. We know that we are not alone, you are with us continually.

All people recognize that graven images made by man are flawed and possess no power. This nation cherishes the direct connection we have with you through Christ.

Thank you, Lord, that our relationship is not with wood or paint or porcelain. We have a living God who is before and beside us each moment.

The world understands that rituals do not give purity or strength to worshipers. All nations deny false gods and choose to worship I AM, the living God.

You are a God who does not need a physical representation to make yourself known. Your power and presence are felt throughout the earth. All see you as the only true God.

His presence

False gods

Other religions

Beliefs that are safe and convenient

Illusion

Symbols from all religions

Heaven

Reliance on God

Man-made vs. God-made

Rituals

Religious texts

Blessings

Monuments

Devotion

Faith

Belief in God

Scholars

One on one

The Messiah

The Bible

Trust

Holiness

Vision

Peace

THE NAME OF THE LORD
Day 3

A name isn't only a label by which we identify someone. A name holds the power of a person's position. It represents their stature, knowledge, expertise, and character.

Taking the name of the Lord in vain doesn't only include speaking his name as bad language. Vanity equally refers to improperly using his name as access to God's power or approval.

When using the name of our employer, we must be cautious to not assume power or authority that has not been approved by our boss. The same is true of Jehovah.

Religion has been used to control and manipulate populations for all time. Some justify their actions by using God's name. This implies that they have some divine power; that God will back up their word and everyone should follow them unquestioningly.

Is Yahweh embarrassed when we use his name as a weapon rather than an extended hand? Using his name inappropriately, even with good intentions, does not exclude us from his wrath or his disappointment.

Praise Prayers

Jehovah is sovereign. The Lord is all powerful. I AM is not a label but a representation of your spirit

We use your name with fear and trembling, taking care to speak your name with praise and worship, with encouragement and support. We leave judging and condemnation to you in your righteous wisdom.

We recognize who you are and what we are to you. Your name and power is appreciated in all cultures. Thank you for showing us how to use your name in daily conversation and in prayer.

Your name is known throughout all the earth. Your name is revered in all the world.

Your name is a delight to us, giving us comfort and assurance. We worship you.

Your name, like your spirit, flows around the earth as your people praise you.

Using God's name appropriately

Power of position

Authority

Fear of Jehovah

Meaning and purpose of using God's name

Speaking about Yahweh

The name of Jesus

Confidence in the Lord

Word of God

God's reputation

How the world sees Christians

Trust

Honor

Our redeemer

Respect

Notes

Notes

_____

_____

_____

_____

_____

_____

_____

_____

_____

_____

_____

_____

_____

_____

_____

_____

_____

_____

SABBATH
Day 4

We need regular rest. God commands it. We need a day without work, physical or spiritual.

We have become so busy that we often put Jehovah and rest aside to manage the demands of daily life. We need time to consider our relationship and connection to Yahweh, to other Christians, or to society.

The Sabbath is for refreshing our spirit and body. We should enjoy it. It's a time for spiritual rest, a vacation from the battle, a time to receive advice, encouragement, or comfort.

The Sabbath renews our strength, our joy, our center of holiness.

Though Jesus released us from a strict day-each-week schedule, the purpose of this commandment is still valid and true.

For best results make sure there is ample room for the Sabbath in your life.

Praise Prayers

As for me and my nation we serve the Lord. As for me and my country we praise Jehovah.

The Sabbath is time that we cherish for drawing closer to you. We look forward to learning how to improve our relationship with you and to being better Christians. We understand the importance of time with Christ and Christians.

The world sees through the rituals performed by other religions that give the illusion of control and safety. You give us discernment of false prophets and false gods. You reveal true holiness through us each day.

The Sabbath is a time to put problems at arms length while we ask for wisdom in handling them, review a situation, or gain perspective. We seek your wisdom.

Thank you that we have a direct relationship with you. We do not have to rely on others to speak for us. Jesus is our savior.

People all around the world recognize your holiness and purity that shines in Christians each day.

God's presence

Rest

Refreshed

Fellowship

Christian relationships

History of religions around the world

Choosing God

Priorities

Ways of worshiping

Places of worship

Perspective

Community

Rejuvenated

Prophecies

Rituals

Hallowed ground

Mentors

Confidence

Peace

ELDERS
Day 5

Aging

Generations of family

Wisdom

Experience

Sacrifices of those
who came before

Failures and
triumphs of others

Weight of the younger
generations on
elder shoulders

Vision from experience

Identity as we age

The core of a matter

Lifetime achievements

Stamina

Spiritual strength

Hopes and dreams not
limited by calendars

Spiritual guidance

End of life

Career achievements

Fulfillment of God's
plan for us

Retirement

Mentoring

Traditions

The past

Sinner or Christian, those who have lived longer have endured more and experienced more spiritual warfare. Take care to heed their observations, directions, and advice with thoughtful consideration. Humans haven't changed. Dreams and problems have always been here. Seek the perception and discernment of those who have been where you are. Listen carefully to their guidance.

Don't assume that the outside matches the inside. Even when we know one's life-history, we do not know all that they have faced or where their soul has been. Elders need the same nurturing, support, and safety net as anyone else. Growing older does not automatically cause spiritual maturity or strength. Elders have the same needs as those who are younger.

Eldership is not exclusive to an age group. We all are elders in some way. By sharing our struggles, triumphs, and insights we arm others with tools and weapons for their battles. Our experience empowers others to achieve victory. By informing and arming others, we declare and prove God's power and abundance.

Praise Prayers

Thank you, Jehovah, for giving us elders to care for us and counsel us. We learn from their advice and guidance. Elders keep us from mistakes, encouraging us toward wise paths.

Our country recognizes the value of aging and appreciates our elders. We are guided by their experience and insight. They are admired and respected.

Thank you for revealing to us the concerns and worries of our elders. You remind us that elders still need encouragement and support. We make sure that they do not walk alone.

Help us choose elders who will lead us to deeper righteousness and wisdom. We learn from those who have had more experiences and situations than we have. Our elders offer us leadership and wisdom to navigate the daily life.

Thank you for the wisdom to help those who need guidance. You teach us to show others what we have learned in our life. We rely on you to give us the words, knowledge, and understanding to ease their journey.

Thank you for our elders.

Notes

_____

_____

_____

_____

_____

_____

_____

_____

_____

_____

_____

_____

_____

_____

_____

_____

_____

_____

Notes

_____

_____

_____

_____

_____

_____

_____

_____

_____

_____

_____

_____

_____

_____

_____

_____

_____

UNNATURAL DEATH
Day 6

An unnatural death stays with all involved for the rest of their lives. The killer and the deceased are not the only people affected.

Families of the killer and the deceased, co-workers, even neighbors need comfort, assurance, and forgiveness. Those who deal with death, such as morticians, police, social workers, attorneys, judges, and jailors endure a revolving door of situations. Even the strongest of Christians can become weary, how much more so those that don't have Jesus as their spiritual guide.

Trauma, anger, resentment, and revenge are powerful feelings that can lead anyone to evil; confusion most of all. If God is all-powerful, then why did he let this happen? Those involved in and near the situation need to know that he does care.

Death due to a failure of skill or resources, for survival or defense, or that is accidental doesn't negate the sorrow or impact of a lost life. Evil will use any opportunity to break down a soul or to breed anger, shame, fear, vengeance, or hatred.

Pray over those who are affected by any unnatural death.

Praise Prayers

We understand that anger is a powerful emotion that rights wrongs, keeps us in check, and gives us courage to defend ourselves yet can harm deeply. We are a culture that values self-control and understands that anger can be a poison if we allow it to take root in our soul.

We have the strength and trust in you to forgive those who have hurt us. We pray over our response to wrongs done to us. We use hurts to spur us to good deeds and positive changes in our relationships.

You forgive those who have taken a life. Show us how to comfort those who have been touched by unnatural death. Thank you for paths that lead to life more abundantly.

Our culture denies violence, instead we value working through problems, compromising, responding with patience, and choosing forgiveness over revenge.

Show us when it is our duty to intervene and defend. Show us how to nurture victims and perpetrators to a place of peace and healing.

We defeat evil by turning away from revenge instead choosing mercy, forgiveness, and love.

Assault
Destruction
Crimes
Anger
Self-control
Murder
Forgiveness
Understanding
Power
Justice
Helplessness
Healing
Support systems
Escape
Freedom
Vengeance
War
Dominance
Jealousy
Abortion
Defense
Desperation
Corporations
First responders
Hospital staff
Suicide
Culture
Trauma
Counselors
Mental health
Pride
Stature
Fear

SEXUAL MORALITY
Day 7

Marriage

Adultery

Fornication

Promiscuity

Culture

Pornography

Molestation

Image

Temptation

Dating

Rape

Identity

Parents' rights

Right to life

Divorce

Sexual purity

Test tube babies

Genetic engineering

Fertility

Love

Health

Self-love

Homosexuality

Media

Entertainment

Adoption

The way that we view and handle sex is a reflection of our image of our self. If we hold ourselves in high respect and value, then that is how we treat relationships. Sexual morality builds our honor and character.

Life-long monogamous relationships build bonds that create a fortified society, solid government, secure families, and stable, healthy individuals.

Multiple-partner lifestyles create flimsy, sticky links between people that pull us in misshapen directions that will not hold up under strain or time. This creates unsupported structures that will collapse, trapping some inside a sinkhole while tossing others far away.

Marriage is a well-built structure that can weather a heavy storm but fornication and adultery are tattered tents that will blow away in a light shower. Marriage builds strong columns that support a family's character and soul but fornication crumbles the foundation of psyche and self.

Choosing a life-long commitment requires careful observation and understanding of one's self. More than any other decision, marriage needs the most reflection and consideration. It's better to be alone than with the wrong person. Choose carefully.

Praise Prayers

We praise the Lord that self-control and sexual faithfulness is regarded as honorable. Our culture appreciates and values sexual morality.

Couples choose to wait until they are married to engage in sexual relations, preferring to respect themselves and their relationship.

Our society values and promotes safety for all. We praise the Lord for a reduction in sexual crimes. You heal victims of sexual immorality; restoring and purifying their soul of wounds and stains.

We glorify God that the media portrays sexuality in a healthy, honorable light that encourages purity and faithfulness.

We honor, and ensure, our future spouse by keeping ourselves clean and pure, waiting for a relationship that will be a good match throughout our lives.

Thank you that sexual morality gives our culture stability and recognition of the things that are of great importance in our lives. We cherish your holiness.

Notes

Notes

SHALT NOT STEAL
Day 8

While our soul is made of spirit, as humans we are bound by physical needs. Our desire is often to objects and things presenting a delicate balance between spirit and physical. The attainment of objects gives an illusion of satisfaction, happiness, and fulfillment but, like all things physical, stuff can be stolen.

Theft demoralizes and degrades the reward of honest work. It detracts from the encouragement of achievement, deteriorating the pleasure of labor. Theft steals the faith and purpose of one's toil and effort.

It destabilizes relationships and robs trust. Theft crumbles the foundations of confidence, creating suspicion and instability. It can alienate from support systems, instilling anxiety and reservations. The invasion of one's space or the loss of objects plants seeds of worry, distraction, and doubt.

For a thief, stealing causes repercussions for years. It decays the columns of one's future. Without warning consequences can collapse plans and relationships.

When we are the victims of theft forgive quickly, choosing to savor the rich contentment and peace that comes with a life in Yahweh.

Praise Prayers

Thank you, Lord, that we have such a safety in our lives that theft is almost unheard of in our society.

Our culture values righteous conduct. We teach our children to respect the belongings of others and to earn and care for all that we have.

We are blessed with plentiful opportunities for all to have honorable work and worthwhile compensation.

We appreciate your grace to forgive when we are the victims of theft. We are grateful for your forgiveness when we have stolen from others.

You instill contentment and patience in our souls when we have less and show us ways of fulfilling our wants and desires.

You, oh Lord, provide all that we need on this earth. We appreciate and cherish the blessings that you give us that far exceed anything physical on this earth.

We value your presence more than we ever value physical objects. We seek your love and spirit in our hearts. You give us contentment and joy each day no matter our circumstance.

Physical objects
Achievements
Apologies
Honor
Faithfulness
Peace
Assurance
Responsibility
Trust
Reliability
Confidence
Safety
Inheritance
Earnings
Labor
Treasures
Property
Fear
Anxiety
Relationships
Hope
Integrity
Generosity
Protection
Purpose
Support
Kneeling together
Defense
Envy

FALSE WITNESS
Day 9

Truth

Deceit

Fraud

Falsehood

Pride

Ego

Anger

Greed

Envy

Selflessness

Honor

Fear

Community

Integrity

Generosity

Apathy

Intention

Power

Control

Christians

Relationships

Religions

Omission

Our word is the mirror of our honor. Our word is the way others trust or rely on us and prove our character. God's word is his honor and holiness in action. The world is filled with people, governments, and businesses who use words to mask feelings, motives, and intentions.

God's motives are pure and holy. We can forever trust his word and intent for us. Christians are an example of him. To the world we are a window into Yahweh's nature.

We are the embodiment of the living word of God. Christians witness Yahweh's spirit directly and reflect it out into the world for all to see and feel. By us sinners recognize the Living God and can choose to worship him.

Even when mistreated we must be trustworthy because we represent the Holy One. If we don't keep our word, then why would anyone believe or trust in the God we proclaim?

He gives us the peace to act righteously when mislead and deceived. We have mercy on those who have lied to restore fractured relationships; giving compassion and grace just as God gives to us.

Jehovah gives us the strength to follow through on our word when circumstances are hard, when we are betrayed, or when we stand alone. God is our comfort and our shield no matter the hurt.

Truth is the emblem of God. Forgiveness leads the way to heaven. May we be an example of God's word every moment.

Praise Prayers

Thank you, Messiah, that you bring purity to our lives. We do not have to lie or cheat our way through life. You are with us each day.

You give us wisdom, knowledge, and understanding to choose forgiveness and to reach with out-stretched hands to those who have hurt us.

Contentment from you is continual. You provide everything that we need.

Christians stand for righteousness in all circumstance. We have your spirit to guide us in all things.

We have constant assurance that you keep your word. Our God is honorable and faithful. He provides for us.

Thank you for the ultimate truths of salvation and heaven.

Notes

Notes

COVET
Day 10

Hierarchy. We have a need to compare ourselves to others. When we see our neighbors, we assume that they have it better than we do. We believe that they have, not only fewer but, easier problems. They are getting more from God than we are. This leads to a longing for things that just don't belong to us.

Desire is a driving force that gives us strength, bravery, stamina, and fulfillment yet skews our perception of ourselves, others, and the importance of an object or achievement.

We can't understand the potential cost of what we perceive others to have. God knows the toll it would take on our family, health, or our spirituality to allow us certain extravagances. Humans focus on the outward. Yahweh sees us from the inside. We desire gratification while Jehovah desires the perfection of our soul.

Coveting causes a distorted view of an object, achievement, or status which then affects our judgment and focus.

We choose to love or to covet which comes from perceived lack. We can defeat want with contentment. Seek God for tranquility and direction for every need or desire.

Accepting who God made us is a big part of peace. Wanting to improve our situation is natural and healthy but consider and appreciate the joys of today.

Praise Prayers

Lord we thank you that we do not have to spend our lives in constant want and desire. We recognize that physical things cannot fill a void in our soul.

God provides us with perfect contentment. You give us strength to focus on your spirit. We compare ourselves only with Christ.

You give us all that we need including the wisdom to see the difference between wants and necessities.

We choose to enjoy the life and relationships we have; appreciating the gentle peace that laps tenderly in our soul.

You protect us from the problems desire creates by giving us contentment. You keep our desires in proper perspective with your holy plan for our lives.

Wealth

Physical

Envy

Beauty

Popularity

Lust

Self-worth

Livelihood

Resentment

Satisfaction

Fulfillment

Choices

Perspective

Achievements

Fear

Ego

Needs

Family

Reputation

Status

Opportunity

Health

Talents

Power

Influence

Identity

MERCY
Day 11

Kindness

Compassion

Forgiveness

Understanding

Love

Generosity

Chances

Experience

Punishment

Revenge

Wounds

Childhood

Culture

Wisdom

Knowledge

Pain

More time

Fear

Ego

Pride

Status

Ambition

Perception

Motivation

Anger

Enemies

Desire

Relationships

Without mercy no one gets to heaven. We all need forgiveness. We all make choices that harm others more than we know. How very generous and kind Christ is to us.

We see others through a prism of glass and mirrors. The mirrors are shaped by our experiences and reflect our soul and psyche. The glass is stained or polished by our choices. We then view others' actions through this embellished perception. Only Jesus can truly understand our motivations and our choices. Only God can see into our souls.

How often have we judged someone without a moment's thought as to how they arrived at their present condition or behavior? When have we spoken against one without considering how their experiences formed them into the person they are today?

We all carry the complications of our plans, experiences, relationships, and circumstances. If our lives were perfect then we would have no understanding for the lives of sinners; their problems or actions.

Christ can clean our soul and give us a wisdom and purity through which to view and understand ourselves and others. With mercy we give others what Jesus gives to us.

Praise Prayers

Thank you that mercy is available for the asking.

We thank you for the Messiah and his example of your love for us.

You give us the ability to give mercy to others and show us when mercy is needed.

We know that we do not fail when we are generous with mercy.

We seek God's wisdom of how to give mercy so that we reveal your love.

We recognize that past experiences can shape our behavior if we allow it. You give us the strength and patience to choose our reactions to wrongs and rights. We follow your example for mercy and compassion.

Soften our hearts. Give us the perception to see beyond one's words and actions to the hurts and wounds beneath.

We are grateful that you love us so much that no matter what we have done you will give us mercy, if we ask.

Notes

_____

_____

_____

_____

_____

_____

_____

_____

_____

_____

_____

_____

_____

_____

_____

_____

_____

_____

_____

Notes

_____

_____

_____

_____

_____

_____

_____

_____

_____

_____

_____

_____

_____

_____

_____

_____

_____

_____

FAMILY
Day 12

The first thing that God does for us is place us in a family. Our family is the root and framework of our identity and self-view. We often see ourselves in the reflection and shadow of our relatives, to reject or mirror that which we see.

The reputation of our family travels around us like a breeze. The actions of one affect all members of a family. The righteousness and honor of one member shines grace on all of the others.

Not every family is formed in a perfect Christian setting. Whatever the circumstance, no soul is created without God's permission or born without God's love. He placed us within this family.

A functioning family requires dedication, a deliberate, daily choice to be available and welcoming. Unfulfilled expectations, unresolved disappointments, the illusions of triumph, pursuit of plans; all can complicate relationships and interactions. Maintaining a loving family means regularly renewing the foundations of support systems that must be forgiving, kind, understanding, and overflowing with grace.

Family is a gift from our beloved savior. Seek wisdom in how best to connect with our family; how to provide and receive all that we need from and for each other.

Praise Prayers

Jehovah, you gave us our family as a mechanism of support and encouragement. We thank you for the grace and challenges that our families present. We accept our relatives for who they are not and for who they are.

Our nation seeks the stability of a healthy family. Our society values strong, virtuous families.

We recognize our responsibility and duty to our family. Thank you for teaching us how to cherish our families in the same way as you love us. Show us how to encourage and support those that you placed closest to us in our lives.

Thank you that we have a stable family who stands together for Yahweh, for righteousness. This family chooses you as our savior. You are our God.

Our family shares our knowledge, skills, and wisdom to give support, understanding, and compassion to each other. Thank you for the shared experiences of our family that allows us to provide generosity and love to each other like no one else can.

Marriage

Children

Relatives

Support system

Identity

Belief system

Expectations

Orphans

Abandonment

Divorce

Duty

Obligation

Sexual morality

Artificial conception

Genetic engineering

Traditions

Heredity

Class

Heritage

Home

Elders

Society

Relationships

Community

Belonging

EARTH
Day 13

Food

Water

Pollution

Natural disasters

Farming

Weather

Energy

Land ownership

Conservation

Ecosystems

Solar system

Population

Animals

Extinction

Global warming

End of time

Governments

Industry

Natural resources

Oceans

Travel

Attitude

Duty

Culture

Space

Communication systems

Militaries

Religions

Media

Prophecies

Our home is an incredible gift that shines God's majesty by night and his grandeur by day. The glory of the Lord is all around us.

It seems the earth and life are spinning ever faster, yet our creator remains the same. I AM is. From the creation of the earth to this day he is unchanging.

God loves us so much that he will take us to
heaven only after a life on earth.
How blessed are we to receive his love.
What is the distance from earth to heaven?
Jesus.

This planet is a blessing to explore and enjoy. The earth reveals parts of God's spirit that we don't see anywhere else. Treasure and delight in the magnificence of his creation.

Appreciate the earth and all that it gives us. Yahweh's true love for us is proven moment by moment, with each sunrise, with each breath. Praise him for the earth.

Praise Prayers

Thank you for this magnificent planet that provides us a glimpse of your glory and generosity. Your love for us is evident in the earth each day.

All peoples and cultures appreciate your kindness in giving us this planet in which we find continual delight and challenge. Your love for us is infinite.

In the earth you show the miracles of creation. We cherish the splendor around us yet keep our gaze on Jesus and heaven.

You reveal the changes in the earth and skies that are signs of things to come. Thank you for the wisdom to discern the unfurling of prophecies and the nearness of your coming.

Notes

Notes

DOERS
Day 14

We can sit by a field full of faith but if we don't plant any seeds then God will not make crops grow.

We all prefer what is comfortable and requires the least effort. Doing is inconvenient, we are too busy, someone might object, or it just won't be fun. Further, it might cause conflict or confrontation or we might sweat. We figure we already have enough problems to manage. Why take on more?

When did God say?
'Ask forgiveness then keep your head down and wait for the rapture.'

Christians have responsibilities and duties. We can't defeat evil or save others by being silent or still. Living righteously involves fighting evil every day. Be an example of Christ every moment.

It's discouraging to work and toil when we don't see immediate progress or harvest yet we must hold fast to the knowledge that seeds we plant will bear fruit. We are God's children. Our works plant seeds that will reap mighty harvests for God and his people.

Praying and believing are essential. Doing is required.

Praise Prayers
. . . .

Thank you, Yahweh, for giving us this wonderful mission of spreading news of you.

Thank you for the courage to continue doing when the outlook is bleak and we are scared. You give us the wisdom of what to say and do and when to do it.

Thank you for the reward of heaven.

Christians are never idle. We are ever singing your praises. Daily we defeat evil and lift up righteousness.

Thank you for the inspiration and knowledge of what needs doing and how best to achieve righteous goals for Christ. You give us wisdom, stamina, and courage.

Our God is not still, silent, or just watching. We serve a living God. Your actions show your existence and power. We appreciate you.

Actions

Courage

Persistence

God's will

Perceptiveness

Tact

Wisdom

Understanding

Strength

Leadership

Righteousness

Love

Government

Employment

Neighbors

Examples

Laws

Support systems

Advice

Mercy

Compassion

Holy Spirit

Trust

Faith

Opportunity

Guidance

Society

Mentoring

Community

POWER
Day 15

Authority
Employment
Health
Laws
Energy systems
Religion
Industry
Mercy
Influence
Attraction
Character
Generosity
Government
Money
Parents
Reputation
Pollution
Family
Addiction
Fear
Relationships
Ego
Humility
Esteem
Hierarchy

Even the least of us has power each day. Every moment we make choices that affect people around us. We have power to be a friend or to give kindness. We have power in our families, at our jobs, or as citizens. We can love and understand or judge and withhold.

How we use our power reveals our character and souls.

Likewise, we are under power every moment. An industry has the power to provide jobs, to offer a good product, or to keep the environment clean. Governments choose to be honorable, or not, toward us. People around us have the power to hurt, speak up, or encourage.

We may feel powerless in our jobs, our finances, within our family, with the government or in society yet we have more power than any other group of people anywhere. We are Christians. We have the power to change anything with prayer and praise. Our God loves us. He hears our prayers.

Jehovah freely allows us the ultimate power to choose our eternity.

Praise Prayers

Our savior is all powerful. There is nothing too great for you. We use our power with care and consideration. We choose to apply power with holiness and righteousness.

Our government uses its power with fear and trembling, ever choosing righteousness in our name. Businesses and employers understand and wisely use the power of their impact on the economy, the environment, and employee lives.

Moment by moment you allow us the power to show your grace and mercy toward all people.

Thank you for the power to speak in the name of Jesus.

You give us the understanding of how our words and actions affect others. We have power for forgiveness and grace, for mercy and kindness. We hold fast to the power of your love in our lives.

The power of your Spirit comforts and emboldens us each moment. Thank you for allowing us to understand the importance of using power wisely.

We understand that seeds planted today grow forever.

Notes

_____

_____

_____

_____

_____

_____

_____

_____

_____

_____

_____

_____

_____

_____

_____

_____

_____

_____

_____

_____

Notes

NATION
Day 16

We are born to our family and to our country. Our country gives us belonging, resources, jobs, quality of life, opportunities, social settings, and safety. Governing is a tough job. How often do we make disrespectful comments, have given no support for our officials, or lack compassion for the difficult tasks of budgets, physical realities, and the constant pressures of leadership?

The goals and actions of our nation reflect on us yet Christians are a nation regardless of the choices of government or culture. We are a righteous nation existing in this land with this people. We are responsible for revealing Christ and exemplifying righteousness. We are a holy people who worship the Messiah regardless of society or the world around us.

Our identity and character are connected by the nations to which we belong. The reputations of our nations define us to others. Belief systems, shared interests, or a common goal can unite us into a nation.

Name your nations. To whom do you belong?

Praise Prayers
. . . .

Thank you, Lord, that our nation honors Yahweh. Our country is known in all the earth for our belief in Jehovah. We join together to follow you in all that we do.

We praise Jehovah. This nation serves the Lord. This country loves and worships Yahweh. Our government pursues righteousness and purity in all that it does.

Thank you, Lord, you provide us with a sense of community. You unify us with a desire for righteousness and a love for you.

Thank you, Yahweh, for showing us the difference in that which belongs to our country and that which belongs to you. Thank you for separating our relationship with you from that of our country.

Revealed through us each day, our greatest nation is your kingdom.

Community

Borders

Trade agreements

Immigration

Federal laws

Federal programs

Hobbies

Fellowship

Taxes

Budget

Representatives

Foreign identity

Foreign relations

States

Enemies

Citizens

Belonging

Duty

Beliefs

Trust

Dependence

Inter-woven, inter-locked connections

Religion

Relationships

Hierarchy

Culture

Generations

SCIENCE
Day 17

Convenience

Power

Control

Manipulation

Space

Weapons

Media

Propaganda

Health

Discovery

Profit

Fear

Ego

Infra-structure

Manufacturing

End of time

Skills

Trades

Pressure

Achievement

Status

Intentions

Pollution

Safety

Extinction

Quality of life

Illusion

Independence

Scientific discovery greatly improves our lives, yet there is ever a need and desire for God.

We go to the store and without a moment's work we have abundance. This gives us a false expectation that all things are available at the blink of need or desire. Our understanding of God's mercies and miracles can be thin and fleeting.

Science promotes a prancing illusion that we are in control of every convenience, health, and need. This illusion soon fosters feelings of frustration and betrayal. How often do we accuse God of failing us when he doesn't provide an instant cure and release from problems?

Have we used science without considering the results, effects, or consequences? Does this create complicated situations that we then demand that God resolve?

We have better health than any society since Adam and Eve yet we still can't understand the human soul. We can speak live around the world yet we often fail to hear God's voice. We can travel in space but we can't get to heaven on our own.

No matter the developments in science God is unchanged and so is our need for him. Recognize physical blessings while acknowledging spiritual need for Yahweh.

Praise Prayers

Thank you, Lord, that we have so many conveniences. We have the most pleasant lives of anyone ever on the earth. We appreciate the miracles of scientific advancements while recognizing their limitations.

We use technology in positive, righteous ways. Our leaders and scientists value honor in the pursuit of scientific discovery.

You give us the knowledge to cure diseases and solve problems. You give us understanding in how to use science to help all people. You give us wisdom in how to use science with restraint and humility.

We recognize that whatever our scientific achievement, you are still greater and still our God.

We appreciate how you reveal solutions to physical issues while knowing that only you can heal our souls.

Notes

_____

_____

_____

_____

_____

_____

_____

_____

_____

_____

_____

_____

_____

_____

_____

_____

_____

_____

_____

_____

Notes

_____

_____

_____

_____

_____

_____

_____

_____

_____

_____

_____

_____

_____

_____

_____

_____

_____

_____

_____

HEALTH
Day 18

We have expectations that as Christians there will be only pure, glowing joy yet after giving our souls to Christ we are still just as human as we were the day before.

For the moment, we are stuck in these bodies. Mortal bodies reveal the differences between the body and spirit; human and God.

Illness in whatever form, is necessary. It reminds us of human frailties. Illness requires that we rely on God for endurance. Its greatest achievement is to remind us that in heaven there will be only health.

Salvation cleans and frees our soul of sin but not necessarily of spiritual illness. We are all works in progress. As we grow in Christ, we imagine that we have attained spiritual completeness only to see deeper canyons of faults hiding in the shadows of our plans.

We often try to heal spiritual illness by covering it up with distractions such as entertainment, eating, spending, appearance, fault with others, or work. Spiritual illness is something that only Jehovah can heal.

Christianity does not remove humanity. This is one of Yahweh's greatest gifts to us. Thank him for it.

Praise Prayers

Thank you, Lord, for healing our souls with salvation and sanctification, then you fill us with your spirit. You are greater than any illness, physical or spiritual. We know that soon we will leave these human bodies behind. We belong with Jehovah in heaven

We worship you for providing miraculous healing and for providing strength to continue when you don't.

Thank you for revealing the faults and flaws in our bodies and our souls. Your spirit holds us dear in times of pain and suffering. We feel you with us each moment. Your spirit glows a light of love in our soul every day.

We manage illness with the peace and the strength of your presence. We feel the power of your love and spirit in our souls even during difficult circumstances.

You help us to understand the struggle, anger, and the helplessness of illness. This gives us a greater opportunity to demonstrate your righteousness and your presence.

Thank you that Christians do not have perfect lives. We are still only human.

Wellness

Disease

Medical industry

Plagues

Spiritual health

Pain

Information

Food

Exercise

Studies

Insurance industry

Support systems

Epidemics

Mental health

Scientific discovery

Families

Employment

Acceptance

Wounds

Livelihood

Heritage

Heredity

Addiction

Trust

Fear

Governments

Community

Fellowship

PEOPLES
Day 19

Cultures

Traditions

Peace

War

Beliefs

Religion

Education

Population

Land

Food and water

Borders

Community

History

Blood lines

Family

Government

Foreign relations

Identity

Interaction with God

Nations

Class systems

Fear

Languages

Society

Travel

Identity

Relationships

God's will for us

Regardless of the culture, political environment, or physical surroundings people are the same. We have the same personalities, feelings, and fears. We are all born sinners; we all need Jesus and forgiveness.

The history of our ancestors can structure our future. The tales of others may inspire actions, patriotism, and allegiance. This can fence in our ambitions, independence, or quest for righteousness. The substance of any culture is our way of life and traditions. Society is the habitat in which we journey established paths.

Culture and society can distance us from the Messiah. Every culture presents challenges to reaching Jesus.

We look alike, sound alike, move alike, this is our group. This is who they are so this is who we are. We belong here among them. Most people do not have the strength to go against the norm, family, friends, or their government to find peace or holiness. How we relate to our group reveals our own inner strength and conviction.

We can't walk with Jesus when we are flowing with the wind.

Praise Prayers

Lord, you have created many peoples around the world. Thank you for the variety of human expression. You give us the insight to see past culture and peer behavior to our need for you.

Thank you that you have given us examples of different peoples around the world interacting with you. We may look different and speak differently but we are all created by you.

We are united by the same need and desire for forgiveness and salvation. Please give each of us a chance to choose salvation. You allow us to see the truth of your love and mercy. You teach us how to approach other peoples in order to present your presence to them.

You give us the peace to resist peer pressure and group influence. We seek your face and rest in your presence. You show yourself to each of us so that we will have the knowledge that you will deliver and provide for us. We don't rely on others to tell us about you. Jesus speaks to us directly.

The Holy Spirit dwells within us. We heed your voice.

Notes

_____

_____

_____

_____

_____

_____

_____

_____

_____

_____

_____

_____

_____

_____

_____

_____

_____

_____

_____

Notes

GOVERNMENT
Day 20

Without a government we would each have to fend for ourselves. Governments give society structure and boundaries. Somebody has to keep things organized.

Legislatures are designed to keep order and meet the needs of the population but when they fail society becomes unstable. It's easy to complain and accuse until we are the one with the responsibility.

Government leaders deal with ever changing needs, priorities, threats, purposes, friends, and enemies. They must feel as if they are walking through shifting sands.

Leaders are people. Just people. Without God they are just as lost, afraid, and alone as we are. Without Jehovah's wisdom and guidance, they see a situation through human dimensions, layers, motivations, and consequences.

Our leaders need Yahweh to guide them through each circumstance. Praise for them daily.

Praise Prayers
. . . .

We have a government that values us and treats us honorably. We are grateful that you have placed your people in positions of power and responsibility. Our leaders seek you first in every decision. We appreciate the blessings and protection our government provides.

The priorities of our leaders are righteous and pure. Every hour our government seeks our good. You give them wisdom in every purpose. We lift them before you each day. The weight they bear is unimaginable to us but you understand it completely. You root them in righteousness with a comfort and peace that cannot be moved.

Thank you that we have a legislature that values Jehovah in our society. Our leaders recognize the importance of laws that are based in righteousness. Our laws and policies reflect our worship of you.

We mark the blood of Jesus over every council member in the United States. Our council members are dedicated to fulfilling their duties with holiness and grace.

You have more power than any government. We worship and praise you. Jehovah is our God.

Legislature
Politicians
Laws
Procedures
Rights
Enforcement
Judges
Courts
Entitlements
Public opinion
Propaganda
Duty
Safety
Trust
Confidence
Borders
Military
Promises
Foreign relations
Medical care
Elections
Citizenship
Infra-structure
States
Threats
Wisdom
Image
Reputation
Power
Intent
Insight
Fear

EDUCATION
Day 21

Knowledge

Skills

Schools

Training

Trades

Technology

Wisdom

Employment

Curriculum

Behavior

Goals

Traditions

Plans

Certainty

Science

Guidance

Discovery

Teachers

Evidence

Ideas

Exploration

Problem solving

Vocation

Achievement

Careers

Culture

Elders

Identity

Satisfaction

Purpose

Self-worth

From the first moment that we have thought, we begin learning. Everything we do is based on learning. Education allows us to solve problems, earn a living, or change the world around us.

God made us curious creatures. We learn from everything and everyone, even a fool. Eve was eager to learn from a serpent about a God who walked in the garden with her every day.

What are you learning? What are you teaching those around you? Always consider the source. Test every spirit, especially your own.

Negative situations are as valuable as good times. They teach us the signs and paths that lead to downfall. This then empowers us to guide others away from pitfalls and instead toward Christ and holiness.

Life experiences lead us through paths of hurt, disappointment, and confusion. Evil often seizes a happenstance as a platform from which to launch doubt or fear then capitalize on insecurities and from there breed anger and resentment. We need good teachers and elders to guide us in focusing on spiritual precepts of virtue and steadfastness.

With understanding we see the true nature of a situation, idea, or action; with learning we attain knowledge; with wisdom we know how to use knowledge. God gives wisdom, knowledge, and understanding to any who asks. Ask often.

Praise Prayers

Lord, please let us learn of your love for us. Please teach us how to live a life pleasing to you. Thank you, Lord, that you have given us a perpetual capacity to learn and grow.

We have an excellent school system that prepares us for jobs and life. Our culture promotes learning, discovery, advancements, and love for you.

We have elders who guide and teach us how to avoid problems and conflict to live in peace and safety.

You teach us the ways of the enemy and arm us with the knowledge and wisdom to defeat evil in every venue. Let us use our knowledge and skills to rescue those who need help or guidance.

Your value in our lives is greater than anything this earth has to offer. You teach us all we need to know to do your will on the earth.

Notes

_____

_____

_____

_____

_____

_____

_____

_____

_____

_____

_____

_____

_____

_____

_____

_____

_____

_____

_____

Notes

FORGIVENESS
Day 22

Only Jesus is perfect, the rest of us need forgiveness. Without forgiveness no one gets to heaven. If we need forgiveness from Christ, then we need forgiveness from each other. Forgiveness is necessary for peace, joy, or Christianity.

Forgiveness robs injuries of their power. It reduces the wounds to nothing but factual memories. Forgiveness restores power to love, kindness, purity, and honor.

God promises us that when we forgive, we also forget. The promise is not the absence of memory but rather a release from the suffering of the injury. The promise of forgiveness is that you don't have to deal with the wound anymore. The hurt, anger, and desire for revenge all vanish. The ugly fades away.

Forgiveness frees us from the bondage of the injury. As the wound festers chains grow and wrap around our soul like a vine climbs a flower. Soon the vine is strangling the flower; blocking out sunlight and freedom.

Let God's love reach you. Forgive and free yourself.

Forgiveness does not change them; it changes us.
Forgiveness does not change past events; it changes our present and future.
Forgiveness does not change consequences; it changes how we view and feel about the situation.
Forgiveness heals the mind, spirit, and soul.

Let Jehovah's smile shine on you today.

Praise Prayers

We praise you, Lord, that you have forgiven our sins, giving us a path to heaven. Thank you that problems and hurts force us to grow in spirit, wisdom, and grace.

We know that prolonged anger and hurt can damage our bodies and souls but forgiveness allows for healing in many ways. Forgiveness releases us from the damages of revenge. Thank you for allowing us perfect peace in you.

We are grateful for forgiveness. We don't have to seek out and avenge every offense in a never-ending exchange of attacks and redress.

We have such a peace from you that we offer forgiveness freely with gladness. By forgiveness we have freedom.

Thank you for giving me opportunities to understand the true sacrifice you made when you forgave me.

Peace

Contentment

Crimes

Abuse

Anger

Strife

Grudges

Revenge

Worry

Sympathy

Understanding

Fear

Status

Wisdom

Joy

Lies

Respect

Courtesy

Love

Consequences

Justice

Wounds

Ego

Generosity

Victory

Mercy

Dignity

Triumph

Abundance

Release

IDENTITY
Day 23

Thoughts

Image

Self-control

Belonging

Family

Community

Country

Talents

Skills

Employment

Race

Nationality

Self-worth

Respect

Religion

Personality

Character

Honor

Integrity

Expression

Christianity

Physical

Individuality

Equality

Fertility

Relationships

Responsibility

Duty

Enemies

Choices

We each stand in a unique position within our family, society, and the world. God did not make us the same.

We see the world around us through a prism of our feelings, ideas, experiences, personality, character, and values. We view others by reflecting them in our mirror but only God can perceive our true nature and soul. Everywhere we go, everything we do or say is done while looking through the windows of our soul.

We all need a strong sense of self-worth and belonging to stabilize us and keep us grounded. The framework of our character is built by experiences, teachings, and relationships. Friendships and family are support beams of our precepts and values.

Our reputation is an echo of our past actions. It can cast a long shadow or shine a light across our future.

Our mission is specific to each of us. Jehovah gives us a vision that illuminates a path that is unique to us.

We see ourselves as the sum of our culture, family, or choices yet in God's eyes we are the sum of his purpose and love for us.

Praise Prayers

We praise you, Yahweh, that we have confidence and assurance that every moment of our lives is very important to you, that every hurt or worry is felt by you.

We remain confident and content in who you created us to be; delighting always in your will for us.

Thank you that our individual mission is different, revealing how our priorities and duties are different.

You fill each of us with talents and a personality all our own. We accept that our faults and the problems in our lives are not your failings. You want only the best for each of us.

You guide the use of our abilities and mission to glorify you and fulfill your plan for us.

Thank you, Lord, that we have a God who values each of us. We are of great importance to you.

Notes

_____

_____

_____

_____

_____

_____

_____

_____

_____

_____

_____

_____

_____

_____

_____

_____

_____

_____

Notes

_____

_____

_____

_____

_____

_____

_____

_____

_____

_____

_____

_____

_____

_____

_____

_____

_____

_____

_____

LIVELIHOOD
Day 24

Everyone needs a living. Earning money is more than supplying necessities. Beyond food and shelter we need to be useful and to participate. We all desire to use our talents and skills in a positive way.

Our identity is often tied to how well we earn a living in comparison to others. We want to show our value with our employment position. When stature is our goal, we lose sight of the purpose of our talents.

For our culture, employment provides stability. Commerce and trade keep society in balance, inter-weaving our daily lives; providing us with pride, value, and collective achievements.

The way we treat employees and employers shows the value that we place on our reputation. When we pay a laborer a worthy wage, we give them and their family stability and store up blessings for our future. When we fulfill our duties, we honor ourselves and the trust of our employer.

Are we using the resources of our skills, our community, and our earth responsibly? When we use our talents inappropriately, we trade money and objects for self-honor, cheating ourselves. God did not design us to give unfair trade for our services, nor to use our talents for the stockpiling of things.

How do we use the money that we earn? Consider your priorities for your time, skills, and money.

Praise Prayers
. . . .

Thank you that we have employers that we can trust and rely on to be honorable. We have a government that protects our jobs and industries.

Thank you for strong industries and fair trade of our products. Our industries give honorable and righteous trade for products and services. Our industries choose manufacturing processes that build and contribute to the earth.

Most of all, we thank Yahweh for showing us the value of our skills and talents. You teach us how to obtain a living wage while using our gifts and skills for your glory.

Thank you for the mercy that gives us understanding and grace with money.

We praise the Lord for allowing us to earn a living while praising you. Thank you for how we contribute to society through our jobs.

Even in our labor we shine your love and wisdom each day.

Responsibility

Wages

Industry

Foreign trade

Skills

Education

Personal value

Contributions to society

Solutions

Trades

Traditions

Craftsmen

Disabilities

Training

Stability

Employers

Inheritance

Belonging

Talents

Homes

Families

Community

Society

Freedom

Independence

Needs

Resources

Competition

Status

Class

Purpose

ENTERTAINMENT
Day 25

Games

Movies

Music

Social media

Magazines

News

Content

Money

Sports

Books

Memorabilia

Hobbies

Food and drink

Family

Advertisements

Friendships

Exercise

Media

Crafts

Profits

Fellowship

Propaganda

Travel

Natural resources

Information

Science

Excitement

Socializing

Status

Acceptance

God made us with a love for joy. It is his joy to make us glad, to hear us laugh. Entertainment provides us with a way to explore pleasures and adventures. It allows us to share experiences with friends and community. Make ample time in your schedule for rest and amusements.

Sometimes, though, we pursue an activity as a safe, fun diversion but it can be used to change our view, to tempt us, to sway our understanding, or to manipulate us. Something presented with humor, adventure, or as a game can lead us away from Yahweh.

Let us enjoy the blessings of amusements with honor and care for any underlying intent. Turning away from temptation allows us to pursue delights and achievements with gladness that build and grow a better society and stronger individuals.

Laughter is a mighty gift. Enjoy it.

Praise Prayers

Thank you, Jehovah, that we have entertainment that is healthy and righteous.

We have industry leaders that are moving away from inappropriate content and activities and toward clean, healthy entertainment. Our culture values amusements that refresh and restore.

Thank you that safety is more important than profits. We turn away from egos and pride to focus on fellowship and friendship. You show us how to protect our souls, even in fun.

We recognize the manipulation of entertainment to present evil in an acceptable light. You reveal the wiles of evil. We do not feel pressure to go along with the crowd in order to be accepted. We have the power to choose goodness.

Lord, you show us when we are participating in an activity that leads to evil. You give us discernment to see the agenda powering an activity or industry.

Yahweh guides us to choose amusements that entertain in positive ways. You created us to enjoy living. We delight in all that you have given us.

Notes

Notes

_____

_____

_____

_____

_____

_____

_____

_____

_____

_____

_____

_____

_____

_____

_____

_____

_____

_____

MONEY
Day 26

Money is a resource nothing more. It creates an illusion that we can attain tranquility or safety by buying things that will fill a need. We begin to rely on physical conditions to give us feelings of reassurance, contentment, and joy.

Humans are beholden to physical necessities. We are all inter-dependent on each other, on the earth, and on Jehovah. It is not an accident that God made us this way.

Fear is a strong motivator. It can be the underlying foundation for the pursuit of money. Outward appearance often masks deep emotions that drive us. God sees our need for money. The same Messiah who gave food to thousands from a few pieces of fish and bread understands our problems. He can provide whatsoever we need.

Our government, daily, makes choices that affect our lives and the livelihood of the nation. Money is used as a bargaining tool, a reward, a weapon, even a means of control. Trade and commerce do much to influence our lives.

Currency is necessary for any society to function but consider all the paths by which it comes and goes. Consider what money is to you.

Praise Prayers
. . . .

Thank you, Yahweh, that money has no power over us. We have a God that can provide all of our needs.

Please guide us in how we spend and use the money that you give us. Let us spend our time, gifts, skills, and resources with care and wisdom.

We praise you for a stable economy which allows everyone to have employment. We have a society that values reasonable wages in exchange for honorable labor, safe working conditions, and freedom to choose our employer.

We recognize the power of fear about our daily needs. We have confidence that you are faithful and will supply our needs. You joyfully made us reliant on you. We praise Yahweh, our savior and provider.

Our government understands that steady wages allow for stable homes and families to live with assurance and confidence. Our citizens use money wisely to provide for the physical while seeking God for all things spiritual. We are grateful for the things that money cannot buy.

You give us the patience to keep finances in perspective showing us what is of true value in our lives.

Banking

Investments

Wages

Taxes

Governments

Budgeting

Retirement

International trade

Trust

National budgets

Community

Faith

Careers

Businesses

Inheritance

Talents and gifts

Kindness

Debts

Responsibilities

Status

Priorities

Shelter

Extravagance

Contentment

Tithing

Livelihood

Family

Resources

Choices

Generosity

JUSTICE
Day 27

Courts

Prisons

Judges

Legislature

Punishment

Police

Public cooperation

Prevention

Witnesses

Victims

Safety

Assurance

Attorneys

Accused

Procedures

Safeguards

Forgiveness

Mercy

Wisdom

Revenge

Trust

Peace

Reliance

Honor

Virtue

Integrity

Kindness

All humans have a deep sense of justice. It's important to every person, no matter what they claim as their personal beliefs. Anyone will become angry when another seems to get away with something, wanting justice.

Justice is vital to the stability of any culture. No court or government is perfect but we must maintain a system of honorable justice. Corruption demoralizes a society, causing anger and strife among the people. We must guard our justice system daily with prayer and praise to Yahweh.

Injustice takes many forms and happens to us all. Hurts and wounds from social situations, problems at work, or a perceived imbalance can spur feelings of anger, resentment, or revenge. Take care that we do not allow these feelings a foothold that will draw us away from Christ.

Only God can see one's soul and know the motivations for an action or behavior. Let forgiveness and holiness inhabit every circumstance and situation. Seek God first when responding to any injustice. Only Jesus is holy.

Praise Prayers

Thank you, Lord, that our government follows a system of procedures that preserves justice. Our government has checks and balances that identifies and prevents corruption. We value honor and professionalism.

We have great respect for those who are part of the justice system. Their ethics and integrity are under constant struggle and scrutiny. We know that only you can understand the toll these situations take on them, their families, and on all involved. Please give them strength, discernment, and peace in all that they do.

Injustice happens to everyone. We turn to you first to maintain proper perspective and reaction; to quickly resolve the situation. We have an unbiased God that sees the truth and the true nature of any situation.

We know that when the unjust appear to go unpunished, you are handling the matter. We have no need for revenge; your peace comforts us in every circumstance.

We have confidence that our God gives justice to all. You give mercy and forgiveness to all who ask. We worship you.

Notes

Notes

ENEMIES
Day 28

Enemies come in many forms. When dealing with a situation that makes you feel attacked, first try the spirits.

Problems interfere with our lives and our mission. Conflict with other people might be evil trying to divert our attention from a larger, more important, battle. Jesus saw through the agendas of his spiritual enemies and asked God to forgive his human enemies because they didn't understand how their actions affected his mission. Pray for human enemies while seeking God's wisdom and spirit for spiritual ones.

Evil puts many obstacles in our path to distract us from a battle that it can't win against us. God can use these distractions to train us to discern his will. Seek God's wisdom and perception when trying the hidden agendas of spirits.

God gives us the power to defeat evil. We are spiritual warriors. Victory belongs to righteousness and purity.

God handles revenge; our responsibility is forgiveness and trusting in him. Believe in God. He will honor your trust.

Praise Prayers
. . . .

Lord, you provide us with compassion for enemies. Our enemies fear you and turn away from evil. We have divine love that gives us strength to forgive all, even our enemies.

We recognize the difference between someone that we have something against and someone who is opposed to righteousness. You show us when we have been the enemy and how to change our ways.

Our enemies desire holiness and see righteousness as a strength. Our hearts melt to forgive those who have wronged us. You heal our wounds. We see actions in the reflection of holiness so we might understand how our ways affect others.

We bring our hurt, anger, and injuries to you, our savior, our redeemer. Thank you that forgiveness heals our wounds and gives us a righteous, unbiased perspective.

You give us wisdom for dealing with an enemy so that your spirit and glory shines throughout the world.

You give us discernment to see behind one's actions to the heart of their behavior. We deny the flesh so that we might reveal the true nature of Christ. We give our enemies the same mercy and kindness that you give us.

Relationships

Countries

Cultures

Religions

Neighbors

Governments

Ideas

Laws

Friends

Co-workers

Relatives

Trust

Forgiveness

Competition

Jealousy

Principalities

Powers

Dominions

Allies

Partnerships

Support teams

Patterns

Illness

Fear

WISDOM, KNOWLEDGE, AND UNDERSTANDING
Day 29

Perception

Circumstances

Words

Actions

Ideology

Governments

Parents

Employees

Resources

Choices

Elders

Confidence

Experience

Discernment

Rewards

Consequences

Waiting

Agendas

Motives

Support teams

Purpose

Self-control

Vision

Assurance

Love

Kindness

Mercy

Information

Problems

Needs

Knowledge can be fickle, understanding can be molded by desire or hurts, wisdom can fade. The meaning of a situation changes depending on the perspective through which we view it. Understanding can be hard to grasp when influenced by our feelings and perceptions. Knowledge tempts us to believe that we have all of the information that is needed to make a conclusion. Only wisdom allows us a perspective that reveals the inner workings and motivations of choices or ideas.

Wisdom shows us the deeper meaning of a situation or action. It gives us discernment to make good choices. Wisdom stabilizes our minds while our souls rest in perfect peace during situations beyond our control. It clears confusion to give us clarity of perception.

Knowledge tells us the specifics of situations and people. God allows us understanding of a situation or patterns as only he can reveal. Wisdom gives us a vision of the core of a situation and the avenues of where it leads.

Wisdom, knowledge, and understanding must be renewed regularly. Seek God daily.

Praise Prayers

Thank you, Lord, for increasing our wisdom and understanding. Your knowledge gives us insight and perspective that gives our lives balance and peace.

Thank you that we do not have to rely on our perception of circumstance or our ability to solve problems. You take wonderful care of us, providing solutions that are beyond the moment.

We recognize that lack of wisdom, knowledge, or understanding is an invisible enemy that prevents us from acting appropriately; further preventing us from the assurance of faith in any situation.

Thank you for knowledge which gives us the tools we need. Thank you for understanding which reveals the spirits within any situation. Thank you for wisdom which guides our actions and responses.

Your spirit and wisdom give us confidence and peace for any situation.

Notes

Notes

_____

_____

_____

_____

_____

_____

_____

_____

_____

_____

_____

_____

_____

_____

_____

_____

_____

_____

_____

_____

HOLY SPIRIT
Day 30

We need the Holy Spirit to give us comfort, assurance, and guidance. In every moment we feel his presence and have complete assurance that we are not alone.

The Holy Spirit has wisdom far beyond ours. He sees the entire picture of our past, present, and future through eternity. He sees the spirits, good and evil, flowing around us; influencing our choices and feelings. We need the Holy Spirit to guide our prayers. The Holy Spirit advises us of things that we cannot see or otherwise comprehend.

We are not created equal. We each have different strengths, experiences, and perspective. The Holy Spirit gives us spiritual gifts that provide the tools and power we need to fulfill God's will for our lives. When he gives us a task, he also gives us whatever we need to perform it. The Holy Spirit makes sure of it.

Each of us has different tasks from a different location on the battlefield. The tools we need are not the ones that another needs, even if we are achieving the same victory. Our spiritual gifts provide us with the power to defeat the evil that attacks us in our spiritual walk.

It's our challenge to focus on the characteristics of Yahweh, Jesus, and the Holy Spirit. We worship Jehovah.

Praise Prayers
. . . .

You have given us a comforter who provides assurance of your presence and love. Thank you for a direct line with you.

Lord, you give us gifts that touch the people around us in different ways to heal different parts of hurt and sorrow.

Thank you for your Spirit flowing through our nation. You purify our government and our people. This country worships you. We respect and appreciate your Holy Spirit in our land.

You never send us to a task without giving us all that we need to achieve it. With you we are never powerless against evil.

We each have gifts to use to witness about and reveal your Spirit in different ways.

Thank you for giving us problems that train us how to fight and win future battles.

We praise you that you do not leave us to fight alone. Your Holy Spirit is ever with us.

God's presence

Christianity around the world

Wisdom

Peace

Joy

Stability

Strength

Perception

Vision

God's will

God's love

Intercession

Godly power

Divine understanding

Righteous perspective

Wisdom

Actions

Discernment

The unknown

Fear

Consequences

Eternity

Purity

Grace

Faithfulness

Assurance

Sword and shield

KINGDOM COME
Day 31

God's kingdom on earth

God's will for us
on the earth

End of time

The rapture

Prophecies

Power of God in
daily lives

Visions of heaven

Longing for holiness

Recognizing his power

Purity on earth

Heaven

God's presence

Recognizing signs
and wonders

Mercy

Going home

Grace

Holy Spirit

Future

Faith

Forgiveness

God's favor

Resurrection

Redemption

God's kingdom in the fullness of his coming, the end of evil, the end of suffering; it is joy and peace eternal. The kingdom of Yahweh is righteousness, purity, holiness existing in every soul continually, in his presence.

God's power could enact his kingdom everywhere immediately but each moment he newly chooses to give us the choice to worship or reject him. He doesn't force his power or will on us. We have the option to do our will; to live with him or without him.

Some still don't know his generosity or joy. There are people all over the earth who haven't ever glimpsed the kingdom. It's our job to reveal God's kingdom on earth.

When we forgive, we are sowing seeds of the kingdom of God. We are revealing what heaven is really about. When we behave as Christ did; when we are brave in the face of evil; when we give mercy; we show the kingdom of God.

God's kingdom in us gives us the serenity to fight on through the tribulations of each day. Defeating evil today reminds us that Christ has defeated our enemies forever.

For today we are bound by the limitations of earth and understanding but soon we will live in the presence of our savior.

Praise Prayers

Thank you, Lord, that there is still time left. There is still mercy and forgiveness for those who ask.

Give us the wisdom to effectively sow seeds of your kingdom all around us. We need your spirit directing our actions as you bring about your kingdom on earth.

Your Holy Spirit flowing in our souls allows us a glimpse of the kingdom that is to come.

We have the strength, patience, and love to continuously demonstrate your kingdom. Thank you for your kingdom in our society.

We are grateful that from the moment you forgive our sins your kingdom flows through us, unfurling in a presence that surrounds us.

We are Christians. We are the kingdom of God.

Notes

Notes

WEEKS OF
THE YEAR

WEEKS OF THE YEAR

1.	Washington, DC	27.	Michigan
2.	Delaware	28.	Florida
3.	Pennsylvania	29.	Texas
4.	New Jersey	30.	Iowa
5.	Georgia	31.	Wisconsin
6.	Connecticut	32.	California
7.	Massachusetts	33.	Minnesota
8.	Maryland	34.	Oregon
9.	South Carolina	35.	Kansas
10.	New Hampshire	36.	West Virginia
11.	Virginia	37.	Nevada
12.	New York	38.	Nebraska
13.	North Carolina	39.	Colorado
14.	Rhode Island	40.	North Dakota
15.	Vermont	41.	South Dakota
16.	Kentucky	42.	Montana
17.	Tennessee	43.	Washington
18.	Ohio	44.	Idaho
19.	Louisiana	45.	Wyoming
20.	Indiana	46.	Utah
21.	Mississippi	47.	Oklahoma
22.	Illinois	48.	New Mexico
23.	Alabama	49.	Arizona
24.	Maine	50.	Alaska
25.	Missouri	51.	Hawaii
26.	Arkansas	52.	Military bases, territories, embassies

Notes

_____

_____

_____

_____

_____

_____

_____

_____

_____

_____

_____

_____

_____

_____

_____

_____

_____

_____

_____

_____

Notes

PRAYER FOR OUR NATION

By your mercy we are forgiven. By your forgiveness we are made holy.
The wicked are cloven from your people.
Evil we reject. Unrighteousness we abhor.
With thanksgiving we rejoice. Blessing your name in heart and soul.
In all that we do giving praise. With every sound sending worship.
In your Spirit we are free.
Giving you praise evermore.
Worshiping evermore. Worshiping evermore.

The mighty Yahweh is God of the United States of America.
Jesus is the Messiah, our savior.

Thank you, Jehovah, our God, for this magnificent land, this beautiful nation;
this people blessed with your love.

A vision of heaven is ever before us.
No matter the struggle you are our shield and conqueror.

Thank you for the mercy to live in the wisdom of your spirit.
Yahweh reigns in this land, in this people.

Your presence comforts us for you are faithful and true.
Hour by hour your holiness inhabits our people.

We magnify you. Your name is lifted high with praise in all the earth.

We ever seek your presence and grace. This nation praises Yahweh.

We mark the blood of Jesus on the doorposts of our land.
We declare this nation for the kingdom of God.

We continually seek your face; we listen carefully for the sound of your voice.
Another we will not praise.

Blessed are we, children of Jehovah, people of Yahweh.
We worship you.

9 781664 225572